P9-DOC-434

# GOOFY MAD LIBS

By Roger Price and Leonard Stern

PRICE STERN SLOAN

ISBN 978-0-8431-0059-4

57  59  60  58  56

# MAD LIBS
# INSTRUCTIONS

MAD LIBS® is a game for people who don't like games! It can be played by one, two, three, four, or forty.

## • RIDICULOUSLY SIMPLE DIRECTIONS

In this tablet you will find stories containing blank spaces where words are left out. One player, the READER, selects one of these stories. The READER does not tell anyone what the story is about. Instead, he/she asks the other players, the WRITERS, to give him/her words. These words are used to fill in the blank spaces in the story.

## • TO PLAY

The READER asks each WRITER in turn to call out a word—an adjective or a noun or whatever the space calls for—and uses them to fill in the blank spaces in the story. The result is a MAD LIBS® game.

When the READER then reads the completed MAD LIBS® game to the other players, they will discover that they have written a story that is fantastic, screamingly funny, shocking, silly, crazy, or just plain dumb—depending upon which words each WRITER called out.

## • EXAMPLE (Before and After)

"_____!" he said _____
    EXCLAMATION             ADVERB

as he jumped into his convertible _____ and
                    NOUN

drove off with his _____ wife.
        ADJECTIVE

"_____*Ouch!*_____!" he said _____*Stupidly*_____
    EXCLAMATION             ADVERB

as he jumped into his convertible _____*cat*_____ and
                    NOUN

drove off with his _____*brave*_____ wife.
        ADJECTIVE

In case you have forgotten what adjectives, adverbs, nouns, and verbs are, here is a quick review:

An ADJECTIVE describes something or somebody. *Lumpy, soft, ugly, messy,* and *short* are adjectives.

An ADVERB tells how something is done. It modifies a verb and usually ends in "ly." *Modestly, stupidly, greedily,* and *carefully* are adverbs.

A NOUN is the name of a person, place or thing. *Sidewalk, umbrella, bridle, bathtub,* and *nose* are nouns.

A VERB is an action word. *Run, pitch, jump,* and *swim* are verbs. Put the verbs in past tense if the directions say PAST TENSE. *Ran, pitched, jumped,* and *swam* are verbs in the past tense.

When we ask for a PLACE, we mean any sort of place: a country or city *(Spain, Cleveland)* or a room *(bathroom, kitchen.)*

An EXCLAMATION or SILLY WORD is any sort of funny sound, gasp, grunt, or outcry, like *Wow!, Ouch!, Whomp!, Ick!,* and *Gadzooks!*

When we ask for specific words, like a NUMBER, a COLOR, an ANIMAL, or a PART OF THE BODY, we mean a word that is one of those things, like *seven, blue, horse,* or *head*.

When we ask for a PLURAL, it means more than one. For example, *cat* pluralized is *cats*.

MAD LIBS® is fun to play with friends, but you can also play it by yourself! To begin with, DO NOT look at the story on the page below. Fill in the blanks on this page with the words called for. Then, using the words you have selected, fill in the blank spaces in the story.

Now you've created your own hilarious MAD LIBS® game!

# AMUSEMENT PARKS

NOUN _____

ARTICLE OF CLOTHING_____

ADJECTIVE_____

ADJECTIVE_____

NOUN _____

PLURAL NOUN _____

NOUN _____

ADJECTIVE_____

TYPE OF FOOD _____

TYPE OF LIQUID _____

PART OF THE BODY _____

PLURAL NOUN _____

PLURAL NOUN _____

ANIMAL _____

NOUN _____

# MAD LIBS®
# AMUSEMENT PARKS

An amusement park is always fun to visit on a hot summer _____
                                                          NOUN

When you get there, you can wear your _____ and go
                                        ARTICLE OF CLOTHING

for a swim. And there are lots of _____ things to eat. You can
                                     ADJECTIVE

start off with a/an _____-dog on a/an _____ with
                       ADJECTIVE                  NOUN

mustard, relish, and _____ on it. Then you can have a
                          PLURAL NOUN

buttered ear of _____ with a nice _____ slice of
                    NOUN                      ADJECTIVE

_____ and a big bottle of cold _____. When you
   TYPE OF FOOD                              TYPE OF LIQUID

are full, it's time to go on the roller coaster, which should settle your

_____. Other amusement park rides are the bumper cars,
PART OF THE BODY

which have little _____ that you drive and run into other
                      PLURAL NOUN

_____, and the merry-go-round, where you can sit on a big
  PLURAL NOUN

_____ and try to grab the gold _____ as you ride past it.
   ANIMAL                                   NOUN

MAD LIBS® is fun to play with friends, but you can also play it by yourself! To begin with, DO NOT look at the story on the page below. Fill in the blanks on this page with the words called for. Then, using the words you have selected, fill in the blank spaces in the story.

Now you've created your own hilarious MAD LIBS® game!

# BULL FIGHTING

ADJECTIVE_____

GEOGRAPHICAL LOCATION _____

NOUN _____

SPANISH WORD_____

ARTICLE OF CLOTHING_____

SAME ARTICLE OF CLOTHING _____

ADJECTIVE_____

PART OF THE BODY _____

ANOTHER SPANISH WORD _____

PLURAL NOUN _____

EXCLAMATION_____

ADJECTIVE_____

PLURAL NOUN _____

# MAD LIBS®
# BULL FIGHTING

Bullfighting is a/an _____ sport which is very popular in
                            ADJECTIVE

_____. A bullfighter is called a *matador*, and his
       GEOGRAPHICAL LOCATION

equipment consists of a long, sharp _____ called a/an
                                              NOUN

"_____," and a bright red _____. He
        SPANISH WORD                          ARTICLE OF CLOTHING

waves his _____ at the bull, which makes the bull
          SAME ARTICLE OF CLOTHING

_____ and causes him to charge. The matador then goes
       ADJECTIVE

through a series of _____ maneuvers to avoid getting
                            ADJECTIVE

caught on the bull's _____. If the matador kills the
                          PART OF THE BODY

bull, the spectators yell, "_____!" and throw
                              ANOTHER SPANISH WORD

their _____ into the ring. If the bull wins, they yell
          PLURAL NOUN

"_____!" and call for another matador. Bullfighting
        EXCLAMATION

is a very _____ sport, but it will never be popular in America
              ADJECTIVE

because Americans don't believe in cruelty to _____.
                                                    PLURAL NOUN

From GOOFY MAD LIBS® • Copyright © 2001, 1988 by Price Stern Sloan,
a division of Penguin Putnam Books for Young Readers, New York.

MAD LIBS® is fun to play with friends, but you can also play it by yourself! To begin with, DO NOT look at the story on the page below. Fill in the blanks on this page with the words called for. Then, using the words you have selected, fill in the blank spaces in the story.

Now you've created your own hilarious MAD LIBS® game!

# BOWLING

PLACE_____

ADJECTIVE _____

PLURAL NOUN_____

ADJECTIVE _____

NOUN _____

NUMBER_____

FUNNY NOISE_____

ANOTHER FUNNY NOISE_____

NOUN _____

PLURAL NOUN_____

NOUN _____

NOUN _____

PART OF THE BODY _____

# MAD LIBS®
# BOWLING

Almost every community in America now has a bowling _____
PLACE

because bowling has become very _____ with young
ADJECTIVE

_____ . Most of them become very _____
PLURAL NOUN                                    ADJECTIVE

at the game. The main object of the game is to roll a heavy bowling

_____ down the alley and knock down the _____ pins
NOUN                                                  NUMBER

which are at the other end. If you knock them down in one roll, it's

called a/an " _____ ." If it take two rolls, it's called a/an
FUNNY NOISE

" _____ ." Many alleys have automatic _____
ANOTHER FUNNY NOISE                                   NOUN

setters. Others hire _____ who set the pins by _____ .
PLURAL NOUN                              NOUN

The most important thing to remember when bowling is to make

sure you have a good grip on the _____ or you're liable to
NOUN

drop it on your _____ !
PART OF THE BODY

From GOOFY MAD LIBS® • Copyright © 2001, 1988 by Price Stern Sloan,
a division of Penguin Putnam Books for Young Readers, New York.

MAD LIBS® is fun to play with friends, but you can also play it by yourself! To begin with, DO NOT look at the story on the page below. Fill in the blanks on this page with the words called for. Then, using the words you have selected, fill in the blank spaces in the story.

Now you've created your own hilarious MAD LIBS® game!

# A VISIT TO THE ZOO

PLURAL NOUN _____

PLURAL NOUN _____

ADJECTIVE _____

TYPE OF LIQUID _____

ANIMAL (PLURAL) _____

ADJECTIVE _____

FUNNY NOISE _____

ANOTHER FUNNY NOISE _____

ADJECTIVE _____

PLURAL NOUN _____

ANIMAL _____

ANOTHER ANIMAL _____

PART OF THE BODY _____

PLURAL NOUN _____

ADJECTIVE _____

# MAD LIBS®
# A VISIT TO THE ZOO

Zoos are places where wild _____ are kept in pens or cages
PLURAL NOUN

so that _____ can come and look at them. There are two
PLURAL NOUN

zoos in New York, one in the Bronx and one in _____ Park.
ADJECTIVE

The Park zoo is built around a large pond filled with clear sparkling

_____. You will see several _____ swimming in the
TYPE OF LIQUID                    ANIMAL (PLURAL)

pond and eating fish. When it is feeding time, all of the animals make

_____ noises. The elephant goes _____ and the
ADJECTIVE                                  FUNNY NOISE

turtledoves go _____. In one part of the zoo, there
ANOTHER FUNNY NOISE

are _____ gorillas who love to eat _____. In another
ADJECTIVE                              PLURAL NOUN

building, there is a spotted African _____ that is so fast it
ANIMAL

can outrun a/an _____. But my favorite animal is the
ANOTHER ANIMAL

hippopotamus. It has a huge _____ and eats fifty pounds
PART OF THE BODY

of _____ a day. You would never know that, technically, it's
PLURAL NOUN

nothing but an oversized _____ pig.
ADJECTIVE

From GOOFY MAD LIBS® • Copyright © 2001, 1988 by Price Stern Sloan,
a division of Penguin Putnam Books for Young Readers, New York.

MAD LIBS® is fun to play with friends, but you can also play it by yourself! To begin with, DO NOT look at the story on the page below. Fill in the blanks on this page with the words called for. Then, using the words you have selected, fill in the blank spaces in the story.

Now you've created your own hilarious MAD LIBS® game!

## LITTLE LEAGUE BASEBALL

PLURAL NOUN _____

PLURAL NOUN _____

NUMBER _____

NUMBER _____

NOUN _____

ADJECTIVE _____

PLURAL NOUN _____

ADJECTIVE _____

ADJECTIVE _____

PART OF THE BODY _____

NOUN _____

OCCUPATION (PLURAL) _____

PLURAL NOUN _____

PERSON IN ROOM _____

# MAD LIBS®
# LITTLE LEAGUE BASEBALL

Many future Big League baseball _____ are being trained
\__PLURAL NOUN__

in Little League today. The Little Leagues are just like the Big League

_____ , except that the players are all between _____
\__PLURAL NOUN__ \__NUMBER__

and _____ years old. When a/an _____ goes out for a
\__NUMBER__ \__NOUN__

Little League team, he is given _____ tests in fielding fast
\__ADJECTIVE__

_____ and in hitting.  He can either play in the _____
\__PLURAL NOUN__ \__ADJECTIVE__

field or in the _____ field.  Or if he has a good throwing
\__ADJECTIVE__

_____ , he can be a pitcher or catcher.  If he can't do
\__PART OF THE BODY__

anything, he can sit on the _____ .  But no matter what
\__NOUN__

position he plays, a Little Leaguer learns to work with his fellow

_____ .  If you play with a Little League team, who
\__OCCUPATION (PLURAL)__

knows, you may become a famous Big League baseball player like

_____ .
\__PERSON IN ROOM__

MAD LIBS® is fun to play with friends, but you can also play it by yourself! To begin with, DO NOT look at the story on the page below. Fill in the blanks on this page with the words called for. Then, using the words you have selected, fill in the blank spaces in the story.

Now you've created your own hilarious MAD LIBS® game!

# CONCERT PROGRAM

PERSON IN ROOM _____

PLURAL NOUN _____

ADJECTIVE_____

NOUN _____

ADJECTIVE_____

PLURAL NOUN _____

ADJECTIVE_____

NOUN _____

ADJECTIVE_____

NOUN _____

MUSICAL INSTRUMENT _____

NUMBER _____

ADJECTIVE_____

NOUN _____

NOUN _____

# MAD LIBS®
# CONCERT PROGRAM

This evening, the famous orchestra conductor, _____,
                                                  PERSON IN ROOM

will present a program of classical _____ at the _____
                                      PLURAL NOUN            ADJECTIVE

music center. He/She will conduct the _____ Symphony
                                          NOUN

Orchestra, which is noted for its excellent string and _____
                                                          ADJECTIVE

wind sections, considered by many _____ to be the
                                     PLURAL NOUN

world's most _____ ensemble. The program will begin with
               ADJECTIVE

Debussy's "Clair de _____," followed by Mendelssohn's
                        NOUN

"_____ Song," and Strauss' "Tales of the Vienna _____."
   ADJECTIVE                                              NOUN

Then we will hear Rachmaninoff's "_____ Concerto
                                   MUSICAL INSTRUMENT

Number _____," but only the _____ movements.
         NUMBER                      ADJECTIVE

After intermission, the second half of the program will be devoted to

a playing in its entirety of Beethoven's "Fifth _____." Tickets
                                                    NOUN

are on sale now at the _____ office.
                          NOUN

MAD LIBS® is fun to play with friends, but you can also play it by yourself! To begin with, DO NOT look at the story on the page below. Fill in the blanks on this page with the words called for. Then, using the words you have selected, fill in the blank spaces in the story.

Now you've created your own hilarious MAD LIBS® game!

# CONTEST

ADJECTIVE_____

ADJECTIVE_____

ADJECTIVE_____

NUMBER _____

PERSON IN ROOM _____

NOUN _____

ADVERB_____

NOUN _____

TYPE OF FOOD _____

NOUN _____

NOUN _____

PLURAL NOUN _____

NOUN _____

PLURAL NOUN _____

YEAR _____

PLURAL NOUN _____

# MAD LIBS®
## CONTEST

Now is your chance to enter this _____ contest. Anyone,
ADJECTIVE

and we mean anyone, can enter this _____ contest. Just
ADJECTIVE

follow these _____ rules:
ADJECTIVE

Write down in _____ words or less why you think that
NUMBER

_____ should be elected "_____ of the Year."
PERSON IN ROOM                                    NOUN

Remember, he/she does not know that you think so _____
ADVERB

of him/her. First prize will be a deluxe three-speed _____,
NOUN

plus a year's supply of _____. Second prize is a 21-foot
TYPE OF FOOD

_____. Third prize is a full-color _____, plus a set
NOUN                                       NOUN

of _____. Each entry must be accompanied by a stamped,
PLURAL NOUN

self-addressed _____. Decision of the _____
NOUN                                       PLURAL NOUN

will be announced in _____ and will be final. In the event of a
YEAR

tie, duplicate _____ will be awarded.
PLURAL NOUN

MAD LIBS® is fun to play with friends, but you can also play it by yourself! To begin with, DO NOT look at the story on the page below. Fill in the blanks on this page with the words called for. Then, using the words you have selected, fill in the blank spaces in the story.

Now you've created your own hilarious MAD LIBS® game!

# MY MUSIC LESSON

NOUN _____ pig _____

CELEBRITY (FEMALE) _____ Mia Sosa _____

NOUN _____ library _____

PLURAL NOUN _____ flower _____

ADJECTIVE _____ furry _____

NOUN _____ bulbs _____

PERIOD OF TIME _____ 1 minute _____

PLURAL NOUN _____ hugs _____

CELEBRITY (LAST NAME) _____ Bryant _____

NOUN _____ Naima _____

PART OF THE BODY _____ back _____

PROFESSION _____ president _____

TYPE OF BUILDING _____ target _____

# MAD LIBS®
# MY MUSIC LESSON

Every Wednesday, when I get home from school, I have a piano

lesson. My teacher is a very strict __pig__ . Her name is
                                        NOUN

__Mia Sosa__ . Our piano is a Steinway Concert __library__
CELEBRITY (FEMALE)                                     NOUN

and it has 88 __flowers__ . It also has a soft pedal and a/an
              PLURAL NOUN

__furry__ pedal. When I have a lesson, I sit down on the piano
ADJECTIVE

__bulb__ and play for __1 minute__ . I do scales to
NOUN                    PERIOD OF TIME

exercise my __hugs__ , and then I usually play a minuet by
              PLURAL NOUN

Johann Sebastian __Brant__ . Teacher says I am a natural
                  CELEBRITY (LAST NAME)

__Naima__ and have a good musical __back__ . Perhaps
NOUN                                 PART OF THE BODY

when I get better I will become a concert __president__ and give
                                           PROFESSION

a recital at Carnegie __target__ .
                       TYPE OF BUILDING

From GOOFY MAD LIBS® • Copyright © 2001, 1988 by Price Stern Sloan,
a division of Penguin Putnam Books for Young Readers, New York.

MAD LIBS® is fun to play with friends, but you can also play it by yourself! To begin with, DO NOT look at the story on the page below. Fill in the blanks on this page with the words called for. Then, using the words you have selected, fill in the blank spaces in the story.

Now you've created your own hilarious MAD LIBS® game!

# THE FARMER

PLURAL NOUN _____

NOUN _____

PLURAL NOUN _____

ADJECTIVE _____

PLURAL NOUN _____

ADJECTIVE _____

TYPE OF LIQUID _____

PLURAL NOUN _____

NOUN _____

PLURAL NOUN _____

ADJECTIVE _____

# MAD LIBS®
# THE FARMER

Farmers work very hard planting wheat and _____. They
_____PLURAL NOUN_____

begin by plowing their _____, and if they don't have a
_____NOUN

tractor, they use _____. Then they plant _____
_____PLURAL NOUN_____ADJECTIVE

seeds, and by the next Fall, they have many acres of _____.
_____PLURAL NOUN

Tomatoes are harder to raise. They grow on _____ bushes
_____ADJECTIVE

and the farmer sprays them with _____ to keep the bugs
_____TYPE OF LIQUID

off. The easiest things to grow are green _____, but the
_____PLURAL NOUN

farmer must be very careful to make sure worms don't get into his

_____. Farmers also raise onions, cabbages, lettuce, and
____NOUN

_____. But no matter what they grow, farmers really lead
PLURAL NOUN

a/an _____ life.
_____ADJECTIVE

MAD LIBS® is fun to play with friends, but you can also play it by yourself! To begin with, DO NOT look at the story on the page below. Fill in the blanks on this page with the words called for. Then, using the words you have selected, fill in the blank spaces in the story.

Now you've created your own hilarious MAD LIBS® game!

# HISTORY OF
# A FAMOUS INVENTION

NOUN _____

ADJECTIVE _____

FAMOUS PERSON _____

ANOTHER FAMOUS PERSON _____

NOUN _____

PLURAL NOUN _____

EXCLAMATION _____

NOUN _____

ADJECTIVE _____

PLURAL NOUN _____

NOUN _____

TYPE OF FOOD (PLURAL) _____

TYPE OF LIQUID _____

NOUN _____

ADJECTIVE _____

NUMBER _____

ADVERB _____

# MAD LIBS®
# HISTORY OF
# A FAMOUS INVENTION

The first electric _____ was invented in 1904 by a/an
                          NOUN

_____ young man named _____. He and his
      ADJECTIVE                              FAMOUS PERSON

brother _____ ran a small _____ repair shop,
        ANOTHER FAMOUS PERSON                  NOUN

and in their spare time they studied _____. When they
                                          PLURAL NOUN

started work on their invention, everyone said, "_____!
                                                       EXCLAMATION

You'll never get it off the _____." But they built a/an
                                   NOUN

_____ model out of old _____ and a used _____.
   ADJECTIVE                    PLURAL NOUN              NOUN

The model worked fine, and in ten minutes it toasted 24 slices of

_____. It also used up two gallons of _____
TYPE OF FOOD (PLURAL)                                 TYPE OF LIQUID

an hour, and the top converted into a/an _____. They sold the
                                              NOUN

patent to a/an _____ millionaire for _____ dollars and
                    ADJECTIVE                          NUMBER

lived _____ ever after.
           ADVERB

From GOOFY MAD LIBS® • Copyright © 2001, 1988 by Price Stern Sloan,
a division of Penguin Putnam Books for Young Readers, New York.

MAD LIBS® is fun to play with friends, but you can also play it by yourself! To begin with, DO NOT look at the story on the page below. Fill in the blanks on this page with the words called for. Then, using the words you have selected, fill in the blank spaces in the story.

Now you've created your own hilarious MAD LIBS® game!

# GEORGE WASHINGTON

NOUN _____

ADJECTIVE_____

ADJECTIVE_____

NOUN _____

NOUN _____

EXCLAMATION_____

VERB (PAST TENSE)_____

NOUN _____

NOUN _____

NOUN _____

NOUN _____

NOUN _____

OCCUPATION _____

# GEORGE WASHINGTON

George Washington, the Father of our _____ , was a very
                                          NOUN

_____ man. When George was a/an _____ boy,
      ADJECTIVE                                  ADJECTIVE

he took his _____ and chopped down his father's favorite
                 NOUN

cherry _____ . " _____ !" said his father. "Who
            NOUN              EXCLAMATION

has _____ my _____ ?" Then he saw George
      VERB (PAST TENSE)        NOUN

holding a sharp _____ in his hand. "Father," said George,
                     NOUN

"I cannot tell a lie. I did it with my little _____ ." His father
                                                  NOUN

smiled and patted little George on the _____ . "You are a very
                                            NOUN

honest _____ ," he said, "and some day you may become the
           NOUN

first _____ of the United States."
          OCCUPATION

MAD LIBS® is fun to play with friends, but you can also play it by yourself! To begin with, DO NOT look at the story on the page below. Fill in the blanks on this page with the words called for. Then, using the words you have selected, fill in the blank spaces in the story.

Now you've created your own hilarious MAD LIBS® game!

# THE AMAZING RANDY

PLURAL NOUN _____

NOUN _____

NOUN _____

NOUN _____

ANIMAL _____

NOUN _____

NOUN _____

ADJECTIVE _____

NOUN _____

ADJECTIVE _____

TYPE OF LIQUID _____

ANOTHER TYPE OF LIQUID _____

ADJECTIVE _____

NOUN _____

FUNNY WORD _____

# MAD☺LIBS®
# THE AMAZING RANDY

Recently on TV, I saw an amazing magician and escape artist. Both of

his _____ were laced up in a straitjacket, and he was
      PLURAL NOUN

suspended by a/an _____ 60 feet in the air over a busy
          NOUN

_____. And he escaped! A man who can do that must be a real
NOUN

_____. I saw a magician once who put a/an _____
NOUN                ANIMAL

in a/an _____ and then waved his magic _____ and
      NOUN           NOUN

made it disappear. I saw another _____ magician who sawed
         ADJECTIVE

a beautiful _____ in half right on the stage. If you practice hard,
    NOUN

there are several _____ magic tricks you can learn to do. For
      ADJECTIVE

instance, you can learn how to take a glass of _____ and
         TYPE OF LIQUID

turn it into _____. Or you can wave a/an _____
  ANOTHER TYPE OF LIQUID        ADJECTIVE

wand in the air and make it turn into a red _____. All you have
        NOUN

to do is memorize the secret magic word, "_____."
         FUNNY WORD

MAD LIBS® is fun to play with friends, but you can also play it by yourself! To begin with, DO NOT look at the story on the page below. Fill in the blanks on this page with the words called for. Then, using the words you have selected, fill in the blank spaces in the story.

Now you've created your own hilarious MAD LIBS® game!

# A CHARMING STORY WITH A HAPPY ENDING

NOUN _____

ADJECTIVE _____

PLURAL NOUN _____

ADJECTIVE _____

PLURAL NOUN _____

ADJECTIVE _____

PLURAL NOUN _____

EXCLAMATION _____

VERB _____

VERB _____

NOUN _____

PLURAL NOUN _____

NOUN _____

VERB (PAST TENSE) _____

ADJECTIVE _____

# A CHARMING STORY
# WITH A HAPPY ENDING

Once upon a/an _____ , there were three little pigs. The
NOUN

first little pig was very _____ , and he built a house for
ADJECTIVE

himself out of _____ . The second little pig was
PLURAL NOUN

_____ , and he built a house out of _____ . But
ADJECTIVE                                PLURAL NOUN

the third little pig was very _____ , and he built his house
ADJECTIVE

out of genuine _____ . Well one day, a mean old wolf
PLURAL NOUN

came along and saw the houses. "_____ !" he said. "I'll
EXCLAMATION

_____ and I'll _____ and I'll blow your house
VERB              VERB

down." And he blew down the first little pig's _____ and
NOUN

the second little pig's _____ . The two little pigs ran
PLURAL NOUN

to the third pig's house. Thereupon, the wolf began blowing, but he

couldn't blow down the third little pig's _____ house. So he
NOUN

_____ off into the forest, and the three little _____
VERB (PAST TENSE)                                        ADJECTIVE

pigs moved to Chicago and went into the sausage business.

From GOOFY MAD LIBS® • Copyright © 2001, 1988 by Price Stern Sloan,
a division of Penguin Putnam Books for Young Readers, New York.

MAD LIBS® is fun to play with friends, but you can also play it by yourself! To begin with, DO NOT look at the story on the page below. Fill in the blanks on this page with the words called for. Then, using the words you have selected, fill in the blank spaces in the story.

Now you've created your own hilarious MAD LIBS® game!

# WEATHER REPORT

PLURAL NOUN _____

NUMBER _____

ADJECTIVE_____

ADJECTIVE_____

ADVERB_____

ADJECTIVE_____

GEOGRAPHICAL LOCATION _____

ADJECTIVE_____

ANOTHER GEOGRAPHICAL LOCATION _____

ADJECTIVE_____

ADJECTIVE_____

ADJECTIVE_____

PLURAL NOUN _____

ARTICLE OF CLOTHING _____

ANOTHER ARTICLE OF CLOTHING_____

# MAD LIBS®
# WEATHER REPORT

Good evening, ladies and _____. Let's take a look at the
                           PLURAL NOUN

weather picture. Right now the temperature is _____ degrees
                                                NUMBER

and there are _____ winds coming from the west. However,
               ADJECTIVE

according to a report just received, a/an _____ front is moving
                                            ADJECTIVE

down from Canada. This _____ moving mass of _____
                         ADVERB                    ADJECTIVE

air is headed directly for _____ and should result in
                           GEOGRAPHICAL LOCATION

a/an _____ pressure area over _____
       ADJECTIVE                     ANOTHER GEOGRAPHICAL LOCATION

by early morning. Tomorrow we can expect temperatures in the

_____ forties. Also, it will generally be _____ and
   ADJECTIVE                                            ADJECTIVE

_____ with a chance of scattered _____ near the coast.
 ADJECTIVE                                PLURAL NOUN

If you are going out, be sure and wear your _____
                                             ARTICLE OF CLOTHING

and a heavier _____, just in case.
               ANOTHER ARTICLE OF CLOTHING

MAD LIBS® is fun to play with friends, but you can also play it by yourself! To begin with, DO NOT look at the story on the page below. Fill in the blanks on this page with the words called for. Then, using the words you have selected, fill in the blank spaces in the story.

Now you've created your own hilarious MAD LIBS® game!

# INDIA

ADJECTIVE_____

PLURAL NOUN _____

PLACE _____

ADJECTIVE_____

PLURAL NOUN _____

PLURAL NOUN _____

PLURAL NOUN _____

NOUN _____

ADVERB_____

ADJECTIVE_____

NOUN _____

PLURAL NOUN _____

# MAD LIBS®
# INDIA

India is a very _____ country located almost directly across
                ADJECTIVE

the world from the United _____ of America. India is
                    PLURAL NOUN

bounded on the north by _____ and on the south by the
                  PLACE

_____ Ocean. Indian women are very beautiful and wear a
   ADJECTIVE

lot of large _____ on their arms and often wear large strings
        PLURAL NOUN

of _____ around their necks. They have many religious sects,
  PLURAL NOUN

including Hindus, Brahmin, Muslims, and _____. Many
                       PLURAL NOUN

Indians regard the cow as a sacred _____, and cows are
                    NOUN

allowed to wander _____ about the streets. One Indian caste
           ADVERB

is called the Untouchables. The _____ Untouchables sit in
                ADJECTIVE

the city _____ and beg tourists to give them _____.
    NOUN                            PLURAL NOUN

MAD LIBS® is fun to play with friends, but you can also play it by yourself! To begin with, DO NOT look at the story on the page below. Fill in the blanks on this page with the words called for. Then, using the words you have selected, fill in the blank spaces in the story.

Now you've created your own hilarious MAD LIBS® game!

# IRELAND

PLACE _____

PLURAL NOUN _____

ADJECTIVE _____

PLURAL NOUN _____

NOUN _____

PLURAL NOUN _____

PLURAL NOUN _____

NOUN _____

NOUN _____

ANOTHER PLACE _____

PLURAL NOUN _____

PLURAL NOUN _____

# MAD LIBS®
## IRELAND

Ireland is a beautiful green island lying directly west of _____ .
                                                            PLACE

In 250 B.C., Ireland was inhabited by short, dark _____ who
                                                  PLURAL NOUN

were later called "Picts." They intermarried with _____ Vikings
                                                   ADJECTIVE

and with Celts who were _____ from Northern Europe.
                        PLURAL NOUN

In 1846, a blight ruined the _____ crop in Ireland, and
                             NOUN

over a million Irishmen migrated to the United States.  Many of their

descendants have become very important American _____ .
                                                 PLURAL NOUN

The Irish are noted for their poetry and songs.  Some of these Irish

songs are: "When Irish _____ are Smiling," "Did Your
                       PLURAL NOUN

_____ Come from Ireland?," and "McNamara's _____ ."
NOUN                                               NOUN

Thousands of American tourists go to Ireland every year to visit its

capital, _____ , and buy Irish linen _____
         ANOTHER PLACE                        PLURAL NOUN

and see the beautiful _____ and lakes.
                      PLURAL NOUN

MAD LIBS® is fun to play with friends, but you can also play it by yourself! To begin with, DO NOT look at the story on the page below. Fill in the blanks on this page with the words called for. Then, using the words you have selected, fill in the blank spaces in the story.

Now you've created your own hilarious MAD LIBS® game!

# TARZAN

ADJECTIVE _____

PLURAL NOUN _____

ANIMAL _____

ADJECTIVE _____

PLACE _____

TYPE OF FOOD (PLURAL) _____

NOUN _____

FUNNY NOISE _____

ADJECTIVE _____

ANOTHER ANIMAL _____

ADJECTIVE _____

PLURAL NOUN _____

PERSON IN ROOM _____

# MAD LIBS®
## TARZAN

One of the most _____ characters in fiction is called "Tarzan
<br>ADJECTIVE

of the _____." Tarzan was raised by a/an _____
<br>PLURAL NOUN    ANIMAL

and lives in a/an _____ jungle in the heart of darkest
<br>ADJECTIVE

_____ . He spends most of his time eating _____
<br>PLACE    TYPE OF FOOD (PLURAL)

and swinging from tree to _____ . Whenever he gets angry, he
<br>NOUN

beats on his chest and says, "_____!" This is his war cry.
<br>FUNNY NOISE

Tarzan always dresses in _____ shorts made from the skin
<br>ADJECTIVE

of a/an _____, and his best friend is a/an _____
<br>ANOTHER ANIMAL    ADJECTIVE

chimpanzee named Cheetah. He is supposed to be able to speak to

elephants and _____. In the movies, Tarzan is played by
<br>PLURAL NOUN

_____ .
<br>PERSON IN ROOM

From GOOFY MAD LIBS® • Copyright © 2001, 1988 by Price Stern Sloan,
a division of Penguin Putnam Books for Young Readers, New York.

MAD LIBS® is fun to play with friends, but you can also play it by yourself! To begin with, DO NOT look at the story on the page below. Fill in the blanks on this page with the words called for. Then, using the words you have selected, fill in the blank spaces in the story.

Now you've created your own hilarious MAD LIBS® game!

# DOGS

NOUN _____

ADJECTIVE _____

ADJECTIVE _____

NOUN _____

NOUN _____

ADVERB _____

NOUN _____

NOUN _____

COLOR _____

ADJECTIVE _____

ADJECTIVE _____

NUMBER _____

ADJECTIVE _____

PLURAL NOUN _____

ADJECTIVE _____

NOUN _____

# MAD LIBS®
# DOGS

It has often been said that "a dog is man's best _____." Dogs
<u>NOUN</u>

are very _____ and can be taught many _____
<u>ADJECTIVE</u> <u>ADJECTIVE</u>

tricks. A dog can be trained to carry a/an _____ in his mouth.
<u>NOUN</u>

And if you throw this _____, he will run and fetch it. Dogs
<u>NOUN</u>

will also bark _____ if someone tries to break into your
<u>ADVERB</u>

_____ during the night. One of the most popular canine pets
<u>NOUN</u>

today is the _____ Spaniel. Spaniels have curly _____
<u>NOUN</u> <u>COLOR</u>

coats and _____ ears. They also have very _____
<u>ADJECTIVE</u> <u>ADJECTIVE</u>

dispositions and live to be _____ years old. Other popular dogs
<u>NUMBER</u>

are _____ Terriers, German _____, and the
<u>ADJECTIVE</u> <u>PLURAL NOUN</u>

_____ Poodle. Every home should have a loyal dog for a/an
<u>ADJECTIVE</u>

_____.
<u>NOUN</u>

MAD LIBS® is fun to play with friends, but you can also play it by yourself! To begin with, DO NOT look at the story on the page below. Fill in the blanks on this page with the words called for. Then, using the words you have selected, fill in the blank spaces in the story.

Now you've created your own hilarious MAD LIBS® game!

# WHAT TO DO WHEN YOU HAVE A COLD

NOUN _____

NOUN _____

PLURAL NOUN _____

NOUN _____

TYPE OF LIQUID _____

NOUN _____

NOUN _____

NOUN _____

NUMBER _____

NOUN _____

EXCLAMATION _____

NOUN _____

ADJECTIVE _____

ADJECTIVE _____

# MAD LIBS®
# WHAT TO DO WHEN YOU HAVE A COLD

You can always tell when you're getting a cold because your _____
NOUN

will feel stuffy and you will have a/an _____ ache.
NOUN

The first thing to do is to take a couple of _____ .
PLURAL NOUN

Then get into your _____ and rest, and drink plenty of
NOUN

_____ . Sometimes it's fun being sick. Food is brought
TYPE OF LIQUID

to you on a/an _____ so you can eat and watch TV, and
NOUN

your temperature is taken by putting a/an _____ in your
NOUN

_____ . If you temperature goes over _____ degrees,
NOUN                                       NUMBER

a doctor should be called. He will thump you on the _____
NOUN

and say, "_____ !" Then he will ask you what _____
EXCLAMATION                                      NOUN

you ate the night before and x-ray your stomach. Finally, he will give

you _____ advice on how to get well. If you do just what
ADJECTIVE

he says, you'll feel _____ in no time at all.
ADJECTIVE

MAD LIBS® is fun to play with friends, but you can also play it by yourself! To begin with, DO NOT look at the story on the page below. Fill in the blanks on this page with the words called for. Then, using the words you have selected, fill in the blank spaces in the story.

Now you've created your own hilarious MAD LIBS® game!

# SPECIAL SPRING CLOTHING SALE

PERSON IN ROOM (MALE) _____

ADJECTIVE _____

CITY _____

ADJECTIVE _____

ADJECTIVE _____

ARTICLE OF CLOTHING (PLURAL) _____

PLURAL NOUN _____

PLURAL NOUN _____

PLURAL NOUN _____

COLOR _____

ADJECTIVE _____

ADJECTIVE _____

PLURAL NOUN _____

ADJECTIVE _____

# MAD LIBS®
# SPECIAL SPRING
# CLOTHING SALE

_____ has announced that his _____ clothing
PERSON IN ROOM (MALE)                                    ADJECTIVE

store in the heart of downtown _____ is having a/an
                                        CITY

_____ sale of all merchandise, including _____ suits
ADJECTIVE                                          ADJECTIVE

and slightly irregular _____. Men's cable-knit
                        ARTICLE OF CLOTHING (PLURAL)

_____, only $15.99. Hand-woven Italian _____, half-price.
PLURAL NOUN                                      PLURAL NOUN

Double-breasted cashmere _____, $50.00. Genuine imported
                            PLURAL NOUN

_____ _____ shoes, _____ handkerchiefs,
COLOR            ADJECTIVE               ADJECTIVE

and women's embroidered _____, all at rock-bottom prices.
                            PLURAL NOUN

This is a chance to get some really _____ bargains!
                                        ADJECTIVE

From GOOFY MAD LIBS® • Copyright © 2001, 1988 by Price Stern Sloan,
a division of Penguin Putnam Books for Young Readers, New York.

MAD LIBS® is fun to play with friends, but you can also play it by yourself! To begin with, DO NOT look at the story on the page below. Fill in the blanks on this page with the words called for. Then, using the words you have selected, fill in the blank spaces in the story.

Now you've created your own hilarious MAD LIBS® game!

# COMMERCIAL FOR FACE CREAM

PLURAL NOUN _____

NOUN _____

ADJECTIVE _____

NOUN _____

NOUN _____

ADJECTIVE _____

CELEBRITY _____

ADJECTIVE _____

PLURAL NOUN _____

ADJECTIVE _____

NOUN _____

NUMBER _____

NOUN _____

# MAD☺LIBS®
# COMMERCIAL FOR
# FACE CREAM

And now, ladies and _____ , an important commercial
PLURAL NOUN

message from our _____ , the manufacturer of new, improved
NOUN

ALL-GOO, the face cream for women. ALL-GOO now contains a new

_____ ingredient called "Hexa-mone," which is made from
ADJECTIVE

distilled _____ juice. If you rub ALL-GOO on your _____
NOUN                                                        NOUN

every evening, your complexion will look as _____ as a daisy.
ADJECTIVE

The famous Hollywood star, _____ , says, "I use ALL-GOO
CELEBRITY

every day, and my complexion is always _____ and my
ADJECTIVE

_____ always have a youthful glow." Yes, ALL-GOO is the
PLURAL NOUN

_____ cream of the stars. Remember, if you want a softer,
ADJECTIVE

smoother _____ , get ALL-GOO in the handy _____-
NOUN                                                    NUMBER

pound size at your friendly neighborhood _____ store.
NOUN

**Download Mad Libs today!**

Join the millions of Mad Libs fans creating wacky and wonderful stories on our apps!